ARMY CAMELS

ATLANTIC
OCEAN

February
1856

NORTH AFRICA

ARMY CAMELS
Texas Ships of the Desert

By Doris Fisher • Illustrated by Julie Dupré Buckner

PELICAN PUBLISHING COMPANY

GRETNA 2013

To my husband, Robert—D.F.

*The word "Pelican" and the depiction of a pelican are
trademarks of Pelican Publishing Company, Inc., and are
registered in the U.S. Patent and Trademark Office.*

Library of Congress Cataloging-in-Publication Data

Fisher, Doris.
  Army camels : Texas ships of the desert / by Doris Fisher ; illustrated by Julie Dupré Buckner.
      pages cm.
  Audience: Grades K-3.
  ISBN 978-1-4556-1823-1 (hbk. : alk. paper) — ISBN 978-1-4556-1824-8 (e-book) 1. United States. Army. Camel Corps—History—Juvenile literature. 2. Camels—Texas—Juvenile literature. I. Buckner, Julie Dupré, illustrator. II. Title.
  UC350.F68 2013
  357—dc23
                                        2013007558

Printed in Malaysia
Published by Pelican Publishing Company, Inc.
1000 Burmaster Street, Gretna, Louisiana 70053

"Raise the gangplank," ordered Captain Porter. "All the camels are loaded. It's time to set sail for Texas. Camels, *ho!*"

On February 15, 1856, the naval storeship *Supply* sailed from the coast of North Africa headed to the United States with thirty-three camels on board.

Navy Lieutenant David Porter was the captain of the *Supply*. Also on board was Army Major Henry Wayne. He purchased the camels for the army. They would be used as pack animals in the southwestern desert regions of Texas, New Mexico, Arizona, and California.

"Rough seas ahead," shouted Captain Porter. "Tie down the camels."

Two native camel handlers hurried inside the huge stable built between the two decks of the *Supply*.

In each stall they secured a camel in a kneeling position with a harness and leather straps.

"At least the camels are comfortable," said one of the handlers, a man from Arabia.

"Yes, but what about me?" asked the other man. "When will the ship and my stomach stop swaying? I wish I was back on the sand and not on the swirling sea!"

"I wonder when we will see this place called Texas."
The native camel handlers had volunteered to come to America and care for the wild beasts. The men were seasick most of the time, but the camels adjusted to the rocking of the ship.

One baby camel born during the trip was named Uncle Sam by the crew. He adapted immediately to the billowing sea. In fact, the sailors taught him to wrestle. As he grew larger, Uncle Sam surprised sailors by running into them and knocking them down to the deck when he wanted to play!

"Ahoy, Captain," called a voice from up high in the crow's nest. "Land ahead."

On May 13, 1856, after three months of sailing, the ship *Supply* arrived in Matagorda Bay on the Texas coast near Indianola, Texas. A curious crowd gathered. The camels marched one by one down the gangplank of the ship.

"Have you ever seen such odd critters?" asked one spectator.

"What in tarnation?" asked another. "Has the army gone plumb *loco*?"

Excited to be back on solid ground, the camels bellowed and kicked in joy.

What a sight! The thirty-four camels walked to their temporary home. It was three miles from the Texas shore and was a ranch created especially for them.

A huge barn—two hundred feet long and twelve feet high—was built to house the tall animals. The corral fence around the ranch was made of prickly-pear cactus. It was created to keep the camels inside the corral, but they found the spiny cactus delicious and ate the fence!

Because they were creatures of the desert, the camels felt right at home in the mild Texas climate. Major Wayne used the camels to haul supplies from Indianola back to the ranch, but they spooked horses and mules.

Dogs growled and were scared of them. The townspeople stared and held their noses to avoid the strong, unpleasant smell coming from the strange animals.

One day Major Wayne decided to show the townsfolk the value of a camel. "Watch this," he told them.

"Strap two bales of hay on this camel," he ordered. Major Wayne's soldiers loaded one bale of hay on each side of the kneeling beast. Each of the bales weighed 314 pounds, making a total of more than 600 pounds on the camel's back. It was nearly the same weight as three men!

"How's he gonna git up and walk?" asked a voice from the crowd.

"Now, strap on two more bales," said Major Wayne to his men.

"You're gonna kill him," hollered another voice in the crowd.

Carrying four hay bales weighing more than 1,200 pounds and equal to the weight of six men, the camel let out a moan, stood up when signaled by his handler, and then followed him down the road.

"I don't believe it," said a spectator.

"Well, I'll be dad-burned," said another.

On June 4, 1856, after two weeks at the ranch, the camels started their trip north to their permanent home in Camp Verde, Texas, sixty miles west of San Antonio. Camels, *ho*!

Along the way, the caravan stopped at Victoria, Texas. Major Wayne visited and dined at Preston Rose Place, the home of his friends, Colonel and Mrs. Mary Shirkey.

CAMP VERDE

SAN ANTONIO

VICTORIA

INDIANOLA

"How 'bout a camel ride?" Major Wayne asked Pauline, the Shirkeys' ten-year-old daughter.

Pauline sat and grinned on a camel's back when a handler led it on a walk around the ranch. She never forgot her amazing ride!

"Thanks for your hospitality," said Major Wayne. "Perhaps you'll find some use for this," he said, and presented Mrs. Shirkey with handfuls of camel hair.

"I bet I can spin this into yarn," she told him. In a few weeks she knitted a pair of camel-hair socks and placed them in the sun to air. Then she washed them over and over to get rid of the stinky camel smell. Finally, Mary Shirkey mailed them as a gift to President Franklin Pierce. In return for this most unusual present, he mailed her a silver goblet.

After reaching Camp Verde, the soldiers learned the knack of packing camel cargo so it would not fall or slip to the camel's side. The camel handlers also taught soldiers how to place a saddle on a camel's back to prevent any sores on the camel's skin.

Few soldiers ever learned to ride a camel. It was difficult to stay in the saddle. When the camel walked at a faster pace or a trot, the soldiers tumbled right off. Only the native handlers could ride a galloping camel.

Just as expected, the animals did their job. They transported army messages and supplies across west Texas. The camels were also included on an expedition to explore the unknown territory of the Big Bend area in southwest Texas.

They were hearty travelers, too, going as long as three days without water. Feeding them was simple. They ate native Texas mesquite trees and greasewood shrubs. If no food was available, the camels lived off the fat stored in their humps.

The imported camels met every demand the army asked of them. Despite those who doubted them at first, the ships of the desert were a Texas success story.

On February 10, 1857, the ship *Supply* landed again near Indianola, Texas, with a second load of forty-one more camels.

"Lower the gangplank," called Captain Porter. "Camels *ho!*"

Author's Note
The US Army Camel Experiment was proposed to Congress in 1851 by Mississippi Senator Jefferson Davis. He felt camels would thrive in the southwest areas of the United States. At the time, no railroads connected the east and west coasts.

The camels could deliver mail and supplies to army forts and also to the thousands of settlers who moved to California to look for gold in 1848.

Congress approved this camel experiment four years later in 1855. Two separate shiploads of camels, bought in Egypt and Turkey, arrived in Matagorda Bay near Indianola, Texas. The first group of thirty-four camels landed on May 13, 1856 and the second group of forty-one arrived on February 10, 1857. The camel caravans walked from Indianola to San Antonio and then to their permanent home in Camp Verde, Texas.

At Camp Verde the camels quickly adjusted to the Texas climate. In June 1857, twenty-five camels left Camp Verde to survey a wagon road.

The survey party also included forty-four men, a dozen wagons, and many horses, mules, and dogs. Each camel carried a load of camping supplies and food. They traveled through New Mexico and Arizona for the project. Then they continued to Fort Tejon, California, to transport army supplies and dispatches.

In 1861, during the Civil War, the Camp Verde camels were claimed by the Confederacy. Jefferson Davis, who had originally requested the camel experiment, was now president of the Confederacy. However, no more plans for the camels ever developed. In 1865, after the Civil War, sixty-six camels were auctioned to the highest bidder.

Texan Bethel Coopwood bought all of the camels for $31 each. He briefly ran a camel freight service between Laredo, Texas, and Mexico City. He also sold some of the camels to zoos and circuses. According to local lore, all the camels owned by Coopwood eventually were released to fend for themselves. To this day, eerie ghost stories remain about camels that roam the desert!

Major Wayne, Captain Porter, and the Shirkeys were all real people. Also on board the *Supply* were Gwinn Heap and Albert Ray. Heap was an artist and sketched the camels. His work can be seen in documents about the US Camel Experiment. Ray was a muleteer, someone who handles mules, and acted as the ship's veterinarian.

Two famous handlers arrived with the second shipload of camels. Hi Jolly and Greek George, whose real names were Hadij Ali and George Caralambo, both traveled to California with the camels. Greek George stayed there and became a naturalized citizen in 1867. He changed his name to George Allen and lived in a part of Los Angeles that later became Hollywood.

Hi Jolly worked for thirty years for the army as a scout and packer. He spent the later years of his life prospecting for gold. His grave monument in Quartzsite, Arizona, is a large stone pyramid with the statue of a bronze camel on top!